MEDICAL IMPLICATIONS
OF
KARATE BLOWS

MEDICAL IMPLICATIONS
OF
KARATE BLOWS

by
Brian C. Adams

South Brunswick and New York: A. S. Barnes and Company
London: *Thomas Yoseloff Ltd*

© 1969 by A.S. Barnes and Co., Inc.
Library of Congress Catalogue Card Number: 68-27195

A.S. Barnes and Company, Inc.
Cranbury, New Jersey 08512

Thomas Yoseloff Ltd
Magdalen House
136-148 Tooley Street
London SE1 2TT, England

First printing 1969

Second printing 1973

Third printing 1975

Fourth printing 1976

Fifth printing 1978

FIRST PAPERBACK EDITION 1978

ISBN 0-498-06786-6 (hardcover)

ISBN 0-498-02300-1 (paperback)
Printed in the United States of America

This work was originally used as a thesis (part of the requirement) for black belt promotion in the International Kenpo Karate Association and was personally encouraged by Ed Parker, the President of the I.K.K.A and is dedicated to the Association, to my wife whose help was irreplaceable, and to those who want to enjoy the art and science of karate, both physically and mentally, for one without the other is only half an art.

June 22, 1967

Dear Fellow Practitioners:

The book you are about to read originally started off as a thesis for the International Kenpo Karate Association. This is a mandatory requirement for members of the Association, who qualify for Black Belt. Upon its submission, I was more than overjoyed to note that the thesis was informative enough to be published in book form. Its contents cannot readily be found in other books on the subject of Karate. I wholeheartedly feel that Mr. Adams' book will contribute greatly to those earnestly seeking further knowledge in the art of Karate. It will especially make practitioners aware of the effectiveness of the art they practice and therefore regulate their actions when confronted in a combative predicament.

As President of the International Kenpo Karate Association, I am happy to claim him a member of our Association and endorse his publication. May all open minded Karateists benefit from Mr. Adams' efforts.

Sincerely yours in Karate,

ED PARKER (Sig.)
President

Foreword

The art of karate as practiced today can be traced to ancient China. A pilgrim Buddhist monk is said to have taught an embryonic form of karate to his Chinese students in a Buddhist monastery in China. In 1600, the art as developed by this monk and his disciples was exported to Okinawa by Okinawan students of the Chinese art. The Okinawans took a keen interest in the art and combined it with a native form of hand to hand fighting to produce Okinawa-te. It was not until 1920 that karate was exported to Japan by an Okinawan school administrator and master of the art. Since that memorable event the Japanese style of the art has evolved to the point where it includes many systems.

Meanwhile, further evolution of the art was taking place in China, Okinawa, Korea, and Hawaii. More recently, the United States has become a "melting pot" of all the basic systems and a microcosm of the disputes concerned with discrepancies between theoretical and philosophical Orientation and training procedures. One of the most pressing disputes involves the question of scored points during competition. Since there is little actual contact during karate competition, the effect cannot be directly observed. Anatomical points accepted as vital by one school of thought or system may not be recognized by another system. This type of controversy tends to prohibit competition between the groups and slow evolution of the art by limiting the scope of experience of tournament participants. Physical and anatomical theories generated years ago are tending to prevent open competition.

Unsupportable theory is indeed empty. Knowledge of anatomical fact seems to bear directly on the current controversy. What are the possible effects of a particular karate blow? What tissues and/or organs are involved? Twentieth-century medical and anatomical knowledge can answer these questions; but there is no published literature available, understandable to the non professional, which applies even indirectly to karate. It is improbable that this vacuum of knowledge can be sustained without further damage to the art and its competitive aspects. The novice as well as the karate expert certainly would benefit by a more direct exposure to empirical anatomical facts researched from the karateist's perspective.

I have read a manuscript entitled *Medical Aspects of Karate* written by Mr. Brian Adams, a black belt instructor of Ed Parker's Kenpo Karate. I feel that this manuscript represents a complete, well-illustrated, well-organized, sophisticated analysis of the medical aspects of basic karate blows and scientifically validated targets. I feel that distribution of Mr. Adams's work will satisfy most if not all of the needs on which I have commented above.

Sincerely,

ROBERT CHRISTOPHER TOWN,
Karate Instructor, Biology Teacher,
San Diego Military Academy,
San Diego, California

Preface

The main interest of this work is the examination of the medical implications of a karate blow and not the strict execution of the technique involved. Considering this, two photographs were found to be adequate for demonstrating each technique. In addition, the individual Karate practitioner is certain to have his own preferred methods and theories of technique execution which we respect and do not wish to challenge.

Medical information for this work was accumulated through many years of direct study in the field and of course was substantiated and compounded thanks to the services of many technical advisors: physicians in general practice, physiologists, anaesthetists, surgeons, chiropractors, physiological psychologists, osteopaths and anatomists.

A Bibliography is included as an incentive for the reader's futher investigation. It includes the main volumes used in the research and initial verification of medical information used here.

Nozawa Trading, Inc., of Los Angeles, California, donated the use of the reaction timing device which we used to measure the *total* reflex action time for each technique. The machine is calibrated in tenths of a second. We found that an intermediate student of the Brown Belt (SANKYU) category consistently completed each technique in less than nine-tenths of one second. (This figure includes the time used to execute any block, parry, or grab called for in the technique.)

A top view is used in some sections because sometimes a photo taken from the side will not show the exact angles of body torque, etc. applied in the technique, which is a very important factor when determining the exact angle struck on the human anatomy.

An oversimplification of anatomical drawings is used in many of the sections to keep from distracting the reader from the main point of interest.

Thanks to Jerry Fulmer for his excellent photography and to Ed Duggan for his art work.

About the Author

Although karate is an ancient art, it has but recently enjoyed a renaissance in the world at large and in the United States in particular. Much has been said of the various kinds of karate and the techniques involved. Little has been written of the effects of the many and varied karate blows. To the serious student of karate it soon becomes apparent that karate is an undertaking worthy of his closest scrutiny.

The author has endeavored in this manuscript to standardize the techniques of karate as to the infliction of bodily harm. He has accurately demonstrated the blow and then in great detail has listed the likely injuries that would result from such an encounter. I am amazed and pleased with the accuracy of Mr. Adams in portraying the pathology as well as the mortality and morbidity involved. Extraordinary insight into the anatomy has been demonstrated by the author. It is apparent that Mr. Adams has studied the problems to the minutest detail.

Obviously this book will serve to familiarize students of Karate with the purpose of the many maneuvers employed. The why and wherefore of the actions and their importance is made clear as they relate to the impact upon the human body. Furthermore, a sense of responsibility will be developed in the student as he will come to realize the possibilities of inflicting serious injury upon his fellows.

Probably the most important contribution of all will be to standardize the judging of karate matches. The result of the properly executed maneuver upon the human body is hereby set down. Thus a more accurate system of scoring points will evolve based upon the seriousness of the blow carried to the ultimate. I congratulate Brian Adams for his painstaking research project and accurate observations in connection with the art of Karate.

EDWIN W. REINER, M.D.

Contents

Introduction

With the introduction and acceptance of karate and all its related arts throughout the world, have come many legends, a great many of them dealing with the physiological possibilities of various type blows on the human anatomy. These legends from the past are very intriguing, but unscientific. In this modern age there are still many unanswered questions regarding the potential of a well-focused karate blow on its target. My goal is to try and stimulate a greater interest in the scientific aspect of the art of karate, with emphasis on the medical effects of karate blows.

Naturally, I have included blows familiar to most schools of karate. These blows include killing, paralyzing and partially disabling blows in varying degrees of severity. One must remember that whenever the human element is involved, there is no such thing as absolute perfection. This is why in many of the sections it is indicated that there is more than one possible result, because the blow may be slightly off target or because of other existing conditions which might be hindered by unforseen circumstances.

It must be clearly understood that I have just barely scratched the surface of a subject that will continue to regain its status in the martial arts. I have dealt only with the common and uncomplicated phases of injury that can occur from a karate blow. I have purposely avoided the complications of different types of long-range infection, which may have been present before the injury took place or may (due to the weakened state of the individual or other preexisting forces) end in a later infection or disease. Incidentally, this may account for many of the existing mystical "Poison Hand" legends from China. Whether or not the Chinese knew through scientific means what could happen if certain targets were struck or knew through trial and error or by mystical practices (herbs, tradition, or myth) no one can say for sure.

I sincerely hope that the knowledge in this book will not be misused by a minority of individuals preaching sensationalism in the arts but rather will be used by sincere instructors and students who are interested in furthering not only their physical ability but who are also devoted to going along with the tradition of the art by improving their knowledge of medicine through the understanding of anatomy, physics, trauma (injury) and first aid. The intricacies of first aid are so many that I feel a whole volume should be devoted just to the art of immediate first aid and pain reduction.

MEDICAL IMPLICATIONS
OF
KARATE BLOWS

1

Striking the Forehead

Parry (or re-direct) the momentum of his downward blow straight down to the outside of his thigh. The momentum pulls him forward and down.

Shuffle in (still holding his arm down) as you strike to the area between the eyes.

This technique was completed in $\frac{7}{10}$ of one second.

WEAPON: Elbow
TARGET: Middle of forehead

Medical Implications

I. TWO BLACK EYES would be the slightest possible effect due to the branching out pattern of the deep winding blood vessels in this region of the skull.

II. A LIGHT TO SEVERE CONCUSSION would occur assuming (*as we shall in all techniques presented in this work*) that all of the forces are moving well and in the right directions. In this case, the head would be moving down and forward into the oncoming elbow. This would increase the impact greatly and thereby increase the effectiveness of the blow by nearly one hundred per cent.

FRONTAL SINUS CAVITIES

FIG. 1

CONCUSSIVE VIBRATION

BLEEDING IN BRAIN TISSUE

FRACTURE THROUGH THE
FRONTAL SINUS CAVITY

FIG. 2

FORCES OF A WHIPLASH

FIG. 3

INJURY TO SPINAL CORD

(RESULT OF WHIPLASH)
CHIPPED SPINOUS PROCESS

FIG. 4

21

A "concussion" is the vibration (or shaking) of the brain within the brain case. The damage caused by such shaking can range from almost insignificant to certainly fatal results, depending upon the number of blood vessels ruptured and their positions relative to the brain itself.

Rupture of the vessels in the membrane (Dura) surrounding the brain or, more deeply, in the brain itself, will cause a brain hemorrhage and attendant blood clot. Such clots may cause immediate death or paralysis (as in a "stroke") or it may cause pressure to build up within the brain until "something gives." A really effective, well-focused elbow strike to the center of the forehead would be expected to run the gauntlet from unconsciousness and coma to death.

III. A SKULL FRACTURE OR A FRACTURE THROUGH THE FRONTAL SINUS (a small cavity above the eyebrow) would be one effect if the blow were struck slightly to one side or the other of the lower forehead. If the elbow strike were a follow-through type blow, it would cause the bone fragments of the first fracture to be driven through the back of the thin-boned wall of the sinus cavity and into the brain, causing bleeding there. There would also be profuse bleeding from the nostrils because of the tearing of mucous membrane linings in the sinus cavity. These results will cause immediate unconsciousness, coma, and most certainly death.

IV. A WHIPLASH INJURY would occur due to the quick change of head position. (First the head would lean forward and down and then it would be suddenly snapped straight back while the rest of the body was still moving in the opposite direction). With this action, one of the vertebral tips (spinous process) might be forced against a larger tip and be completely chipped off the vertebra, resulting in extreme pain and stiffness of the neck.

2

Striking the Ears

Parry by scooping down and out (the scoop will bring opponent's head forward).

Continue the momentum of the scoop and direct it to the ears (palms cupped) as you pivot your rear foot so that your shoulders will be at an equal distance from your opponent's head when you strike.

This technique was completed in $\frac{7}{10}$ of one second.

WEAPON: Cupped Palms
TARGET: Ears

Medical Implications

I. UNCONSCIOUSNESS OR A CONCUSSION will occur from any well-focused blow to the head. This is especially true when the head is not allowed to roll with the blow. The palms striking on both sides of the head simultaneously will act as a stabilizing device to the head and therefore doubles the percussive shock and pain. *Whenever there is the possibility of a concussion there is the possibility of death.*

TYMPANIC MEMBRANE (EAR DRUM)
EUSTACHIAN TUBE

AUDITORY CANAL

FIG. 5
NORMAL

CONCUSSIVE VIBRATION

RUPTURE OF THE EAR DRUM, WITH EXPANSION OF
THE AUDITORY CANAL AND EUSTACHIAN TUBE
BY COMPRESSED AIR

FIG. 6
MOMENT OF IMPACT

SWELLING OF OUTER EAR

SWELLING OF AUDITORY CANAL

RUPTURE OF EAR DRUM

SWELLING OF THE EUSTACHIAN
TUBE

FIG. 7
AFTER

FACIAL NERVE
FACIAL VEIN

FIG. 8

II. RUPTURE OF THE TYMPANAC MEMBRANE (Eardrum) will result from the large volume of air being forced through the external auditory canal, through the thin-skinned membrane of the eardrum, and finally through the eustachian tube which opens into the back of the throat. The outside of the ear will be swollen because of the broken blood vessels and small capillaries there. Capillaries inside the auditory canal will be ruptured and swell because of the expanding volume of air that has rushed through the narrow passageway leading to the eardrum. Loss of hearing would be from partial to complete, depending upon the total degree of injury to the internal ear. The eustachian tube is much narrower than the auditory canal (the size of a pencil lead), and therefore will suffer greater expanding pressures as the air passes through it. The eustachian tube will undoubtedly swell completely shut. There will be an extreme amount of pain from the double palm strike to the ears. If the blows are not pulled, shock will be a prominent result.

III. POSSIBLE FRACTURE AND/OR DISLOCATION OF THE JAW HINGE (refer to Fig. 24) may occur if the blow is slightly lower.

IV. CONTUSION OF THE FACIAL NERVE AND VEIN, with possible paralysis of one side of the face, are experienced if the blow abrades them against the edge of the jawbone. This paralysis would probably be temporary unless a sharp section of the bone fracture punctured or severed the facial nerve. Likewise, if the vein was punctured there would be a small hematoma* (walnut-size lump) and eventually one side of the face would turn black and blue. (Fig. 8.)

* HEMATOMA: An organized area of blood spilled from a torn blood vessel.

3
Striking the Temple

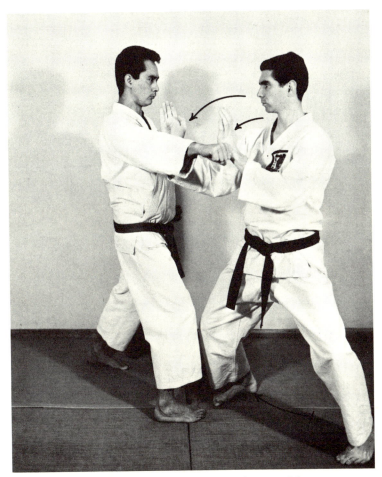

Use a double block on opponent's punching arm.

Grab the arm and pull opponent forward as you deliver a back-knuckle to his temple.

This technique was completed in $\frac{8}{10}$ of one second.

WEAPON: Back-knuckle
TARGET: Temple

Medical Implications

I. A FRACTURE IN THE TEMPORAL REGION OF THE SKULL WITH MIDDLE MENINGEAL HEMORRHAGE (Meningeal Artery) commonly occur together; however, one may prevail without the other. The meningeal artery supplies the skull and dura (membrane that covers the brain) with blood. The artery follows its groove in the skull case (Fig. 10) and is easily pinched or severed if disruption of this groove occurs from a skull fracture.

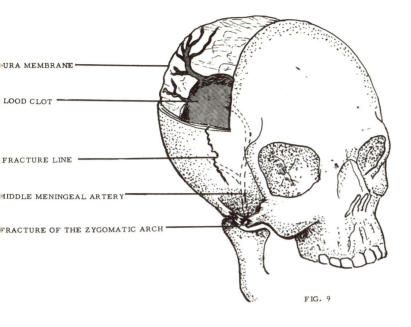

DURA MEMBRANE

BLOOD CLOT

FRACTURE LINE

MIDDLE MENINGEAL ARTERY

FRACTURE OF THE ZYGOMATIC ARCH

FIG. 9

FIG. 10   BLOW UP OF VEIN GROOVED INTO THE
          DURA MEMBRANE AND INSIDE THE SKULL

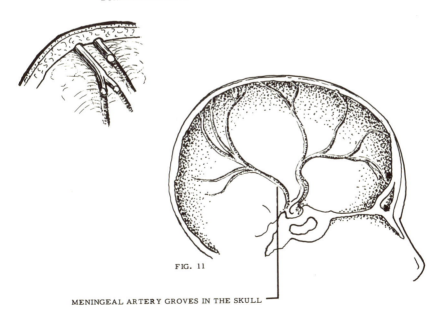

FIG. 11

MENINGEAL ARTERY GROVES IN THE SKULL

II. HEADACHE, NAUSEA, VOMITING, COMA AND DEATH may ensue immediately or may be the delayed result, as long as two weeks later. If the artery were severed there would be immediate compression of the brain due to the massive hemorrhage there, indicated by a gradual deepening stupor. If diagnosis is not made soon, the patient will go into a coma and finally death will result. If the artery is only pinched with slow blood leakage, a small extradural hematoma* will produce delayed results, similar to a complete severence of the meningeal artery. Rupture of the meningeal artery may be prevailent without an accompanying skull fracture due to the severe jarring action displacing the vein from its groove. (Refer to Chapter 1)

III. RUPTURE OF THE TYMPANIC MEMBRANE (EARDRUM) may occur if the fracture line runs through the internal ear section of the skull. This will be evident from bleeding of the ear, nose, and mouth, and also from the vomiting of blood that has been swallowed and an obvious impairment of hearing.

IV. A FRACTURE OF THE ZYGOMATIC PROCESS will be the outcome if the blow is one inch lower than the temporal bone (temple). Opening and closing of the mouth will be noticeably painful. (Fig. 9.)

---

* Extradural hematoma: Blood clot between the skull casing and the dura.

4

Striking the Eye

Block and immediately thrust to the eyes.

This technique was completed in $\frac{5}{10}$ of one second.

WEAPONS: Finger tips
TARGET: Eye

Medical Implications

I. The possible results are so many in this area, that we will concern ourselves with only the more obvious trauma.

RUPTURE OF THE EYE BULB WITH PROTRUSION OF THE WATERY AND GELATINOUS LIKE CONTENTS will result when the bulb is no longer able to withstand the direct pressure piercing it.

TEMPORARY TO PERMANENT BLINDNESS (Probably permanent) is the common result. Tremendous shocking pain will prevail in one or both eyes. An uncontrollable watering of the eyes will always be functional

FIG. 12
COLLAPSED BULB OF EYE

FIG. 13
LACERATED EYE LID

FIG. 14
COLLAPSED BULB OF EYE

whenever a foreign object enters or touches the eye, which naturally produces temporary blurred vision in the uninjured eye.

II. A TORN EYELID (usually the top one, Fig. 13) is the effect of a sharp fingernail piercing an eyelid that has blinked at the last instant before the nail has struck.

Infection following trauma of this kind is the usual aftermath because of small debris (dirt, germs, hair, etc.) that enters the eye with the finger and nail. Sometimes infection can be a more serious complication than the blow itself.

5

Striking the Bridge of the Nose

By blocking you are actually cocking your arm in a good position for a nose rake with the back of all the knuckles across the nose.

Shuffle in as you rake across the nose.

This technique was completed in $\frac{6}{10}$ of one second.

WEAPONS: Back of all four knuckles
TARGET: Nasal bone

Medical Implications

I. A COMPOUND FRACTURE AND/OR DISLOCATION OF THE NASAL BONE AND SEPTUM (dividing partition of the nostrils) are a consequence of all four knuckles raking across the upper part of the nose. Needless to say, there will be massive hemorrhage because of the many blood vessels in this area. Shock and pain may render your opponent unconscious. Temporary blindness may be a result of the extreme watering of the eyes because of the stimulated pain receptors in the nasal region. We must realize that many times the blow may not be a death-dealing one, but the accidental consequences may end in death. In this case we are talking

EXTERNAL APPEARANCE

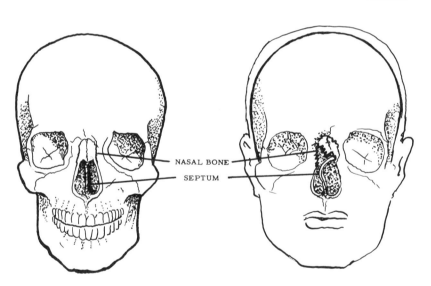

NASAL BONE

SEPTUM

NORMAL

FIG. 15

FRACTURE AND DISLOCATION OF THE NASAL BONE AND SEPTUM
(CARTILAGE THAT DIVIDES THE SIDES OF THE NOSTRILS)

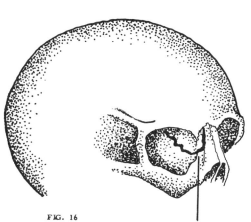

FIG. 16

FRACTURE INTO THE ORBITAL SOCKET

FIG. 17

OSOLATIONS FOLLOW PATH OF LEAST
RESISTANCE AND BECOME CLOSER
TOGETHER AS THE BONE NARROWS

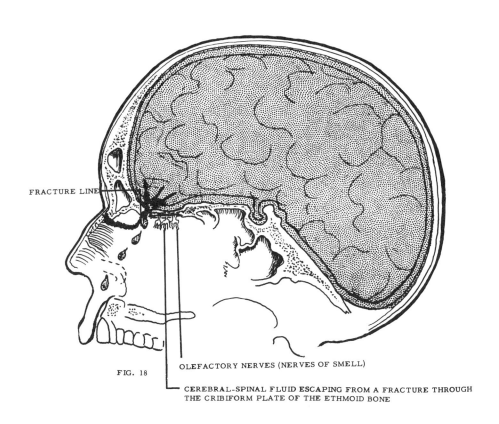

FRACTURE LINE

OLEFACTORY NERVES (NERVES OF SMELL)

FIG. 18

CEREBRAL-SPINAL FLUID ESCAPING FROM A FRACTURE THROUGH
THE CRIBIFORM PLATE OF THE ETHMOID BONE

about unconsciousness which invariably occurs before the opponent hits the ground. The effect is a grave one because the head is relaxed when it strikes the ground and may end in a serious concussion or skull fracture if the surface is fairly solid. (Refer to Chapter 1.) Death may also ensue because of the huge amount of blood clogging the trachea (wind pipe) during unconsciousness.

II. FRACTURE INTO THE ORBITAL SOCKET (eye socket) with possible cerebral involvement may be a complication of the blow. If the fracture line has continued into the brain casing (cribriform plate of the ethmoid bone) , a slight tear in the dura will release small amounts of cerebrospinal fluid. The fluid will travel through the sinuses and finally exit through the nostrils or be swallowed. Cerebrospinal fluid (clear fluid that circulates in the closed cavity of the brain and spinal cord) is sometimes mistaken for a normal secretion for quite some time, until severe headaches motivate the individual to seek medical advice.

When bone (or for that matter any part of the body) is struck, the force of the blow is transferred from the weapon to the target in the form of oscillating vibrations. In the case of bone the oscillations follow the path of least resitence. The oscillations are further apart in wide or thick bone and closer together in thin or narrow bone (Fig. 17) . As oscillations narrow the vibration becomes more violent and causes a fracture through the weakest portion of bone.

The olefactory nerves (nerves of smell) are spread throughout the roof of the nasal section (cribiform plate of the ethmoid bone) and may become torn or severed from the fractured bone. A dulling of the sense of smell will occur.

6

Striking the Spot Under the Nose

Swing opponent's arm upward and across your body.

Grab the aggressor's wrist and pull your captured wrist free (cocking it at the ear). Pull his arm toward you as you chop directly under his nose.

This technique was completed in $5/10$ of one second.

WEAPON: Chop (side of the hand)
TARGET: Region under the nose

Medical Implications

I. A SPLIT LIP, CHIPPED OR MISSING TEETH AND EYEWATER-ING PAIN are the minimal possible results. The eyewatering pain is due to the close proximity of the nerves to the surface of the skin.

II. A BURSTING FRACTURE OF THE MAXILLA (upper jaw) is the outcome because of the spherical nature of the skull. The skull will compress to its limit and then burst, producing a bursting fracture. The fracture site is usually on one side or the other, distal to the point of impact, but

FIG. 19
CONCUSSIVE VIBRATION

FIG. 20
SPLIT LIP

FIG. 21
BURSTING FRACTURE OF THE MAXILLARY BONE
MISSING AND CHIPPED TEETH

there may be a fracture at the impact site also. The simple task of eating may become a very painful one.

III. UNCONSCIOUSNESS AND/OR CONCUSSION frequently follow such a blow. (Refer to Chapter 1.) Unconsciousness may be a result of a concussion or more than likely may be caused by the fast exit of blood from the brain into the internal organs (due to shock).

IV. RESPIRATORY PARALYSIS AND DEATH may develop from broken or dislocated teeth and blood caught in or near the wind pipe (trachea) may cause a spasm of the vocal cords (Fig. 30) with closing off of the air supply.

7

Striking the Jaw

Retreat into a cat stance as you block his punching arm.

Step in with a simultaneous heel of palm and elbow strike to jaw area.

This technique was completed in $\frac{7}{10}$ of one second.

WEAPON: Elbow and Palm strike
TARGET: Jaw

Medical Implications

I. A FRACTURE OR DISLOCATION OF THE MANDIBLE (lower jaw) is a very apparent result of two striking surfaces on either side of the jawbone. If both strikes were simultaneous, a double fracture (one on each side) would be evident. But if one weapon were to arrive before the other, thus pushing the jaw into the path of the other weapon, then only a fracture on one side would be applicable. In order to prevent a future deformity of the jaw line, the teeth and fragments must be temporarily wired together. Of course there will be great difficulty eating and speaking until complete healing has taken place. Dislocation of the jaw hinge would

FIG. 22

FRACTURE-DISLOCATION OF THE ZYGOMA
(CHEEK BONE)

BURSTING FRACTURE OF THE MAXILLA

FIG. 23

DISLOCATION OF THE JAW HINGE (NORMAL LOCATION)

FRACTURE OF THE MANDIBLE

MISSING AND CHIPPED TEETH

FIG. 24

45

easily occur if the blow were near the upper portion of the jaw and were a glancing type blow. The wider the opening of the mouth at the moment of impact, the easier it would be for the dislocation to occur.

II. A FRACTURE DISLOCATION OF THE ZYGOMA (cheekbone) would result if the elbow struck a short distance above the jaw. A bursting fracture in the bone surrounding the cheekbone may result from the crushing pressure of the elbow. The maxillary sinus lies under the cheekbone and would undoubtedly be lacerated by bone fragments from the fracture. Blood would fill the sinus and flow into the throat or out of the nose. The possibilities of unconsciousness and concussion range very high. (Refer to Chapter 1.)

III. THE FACIAL NERVE MAY BE PINCHED OR ABRADED against the edge of the mandible and (according to how devastating the damage) may leave part or all of one side of the face in paralysis (Fig. 8).

IV. CONTROL OF THE TONGUE WOULD BE LOST because of the mandible fracture. Torn muscles on the bottom of the mouth that adhere the tongue would go into spasm and if unconsciousness ensued, the tongue along with the broken and dislocated teeth would be swallowed and death by choking would follow.

8
Striking the Throat

Use a double block on his punching arm

Grab and pull his wrist with your left hand as you execute a chop to his neck

This technique was completed in $^6/_{10}$ of one second.

WEAPON: Chop (Side of the hand)
TARGET: Side or front of the throat

Medical Implications

The results from a well-focused blow to the front or side of the throat are a combination of multiple effects and results. The following is a listing of each separate possible effect and result:

Effects

(1) Contusion of the internal *Jugular Vein*
(2) Contusion of the internal *Carotid Vein*
(3) Contusion of the *Vertebratal Vein*

(4) Contusion of the *Hypoglassal Nerve*
(5) Contusion of the *Vagus Nerve*
(6) Contusion of the *Phrenic Nerve*
(7) Contusion of the *Laryngenial Nerve*
(8) Hematoma in *Carotid Sheath*
(9) Fracture of the *Spinous Process*
(10) Fracture of the *Thyroid Cartilage*
(11) Fracture of the *Cricoid Cartilage*
(12) Possible injury to *Branchial Plexus* (Refer to Chapter 10.)

Results

I. The internal jugular vein pulsates during respiration, distends during expiration, and collapses to a ribbon-like structure during inspiration. If the blow struck on expiration, the vein would be full of blood and hard. Rupturing of the internal jugular vein from striking it against the hard surface of the cervical vertebra would result in a quick death due to a massive hemorrhage (hematoma).

II. Severe contusion of the carotid vein may result in thrombosis, (blood clot in the vessel) due to the vessel wall spasm, which produces a restriction in blood flow. This may eventually end in cerebral thrombosis (blood clot in vessels of the brain) and death.

III. Laceration or contusion of the VERTEBRAL ARTERY is only possible when the blow is heavy enough to chip or fracture the spinous vertebral processes that the artery runs through. Results are the same as the previous two variations in vessel damage.

IV. The two most important functions of the VAGUS NERVE we are concerned with here are that of heart contraction and lung constriction. Since there are two branches of the vagus nerve (one on each side of the neck) injury to one may not by itself be completely fatal because of the partial overlapping of the two nerve branches once they reach their destination. However, damage to one side of the nerve could cause spasms of the lungs and heart, ultimately ending in shortness of breath, irregular heart palputations, and death.

V. The PHRENIC NERVE runs from the fourth cervical vertebra, vertically down the neck into the thorax (chest) where it finally merges into the diaphram. The main function of the phrenic nerve is to supply the diaphram with necessary responses for breathing. When it is injured, the same feeling that one gets when the "wind" has been knocked out will exist until normal function resumes or death occurs.

VI. The LARYNGEAL NERVES (nerves of the vocal cords, etc.) are a branch of the vagus nerve. They control the main functions of the larynx, which are to open and close the vocal cords and epiglottis so that no foreign objects are permitted to pass through the trachea. When a foreign object

FIG. 25

FIG. 26

FRACTURE OF THYROID BONE
CRICOID BONE

TRACHEA (WIND PIPE)

PHRENIC NERVE (TO DIAPHRAGM)

VAGUS NERVE (TO HEART AND LUNGS)

BRANCHIAL PLEXUS (NERVES TO ARM)

CHIPPED SPINOUS PROCESS

RUPTURE OF THE
VERTEBRAL VEIN

(TRACHEA REMOVED FOR
CLARITY)

JUGULAR VEIN TO BRAIN

CARTOID VEIN TO BRAIN

VAGUS NERVE

PHRENIC NERVE

FIG. 27
(FRONT VIEW)

CROSS SECTION OF NECK (TOP VIEW)
FIG. 28

VERTEBRA
SPINAL CORD
VERTEBRAL ARTERY
VAGUS NERVE
CARTOID ARTERY
JUGULAR VEIN
PHRENIC NERVE
CARTOID
SHEATH

LAYER OF FAT

TRACHEA WITH VOCAL
CORDS

AND THYROID CARTILAGE

OESOPHAGUS

LARYNGEAL NERVE

BLOOD CLOT

CONTUSED JUGULAR
AND CARTOID VEINS

FIG. 29

COMPRESSION OF NERVES, OESOPHAGUS
AND TRACHEA BY BLOOD CLOT

OPEN VOCAL CORDS

FIG. 30

CLOSED VOCAL CORDS

51

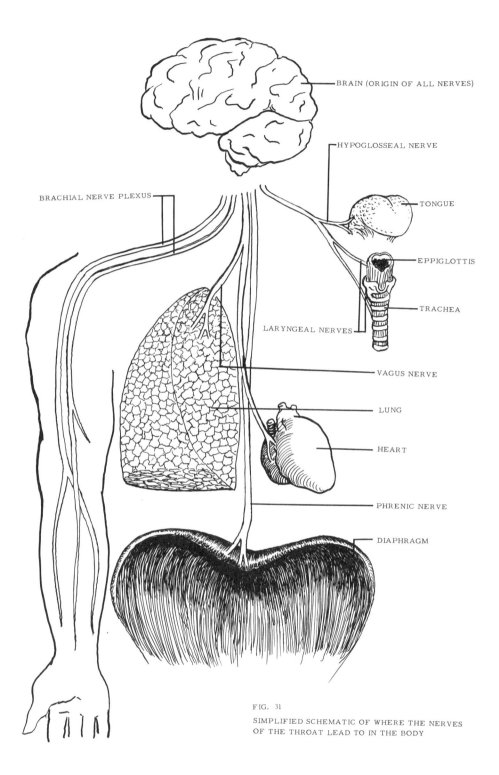

BRAIN (ORIGIN OF ALL NERVES)

HYPOGLOSSEAL NERVE

BRACHIAL NERVE PLEXUS

TONGUE

EPPIGLOTTIS

TRACHEA

LARYNGEAL NERVES

VAGUS NERVE

LUNG

HEART

PHRENIC NERVE

DIAPHRAGM

FIG. 31

SIMPLIFIED SCHEMATIC OF WHERE THE NERVES
OF THE THROAT LEAD TO IN THE BODY

(food, teeth, blood, etc.) agitates the nerve surrounding the larynx or inside of the throat, the vocal cords close and the epiglottis covers the opening of the wind pipe to prevent anything from being sucked into the pipe. When this is done no air can go in or out of the lungs until the nerve relaxes and opens the wind pipe for normal breathing. If the nerve does not relax, death by suffocation will follow.

VII. The HYPOGLOSSAL NERVE is the main nerve of the tongue. If it is damaged, loss of control of the tongue will be inevitable with suffocation and death if it is swallowed.

VIII. A HEMATOMA IN THE SHEATH that encompasses the internal jugular, carotid vein and vagus nerve in the neck is the result of blood leakage from a torn blood vessel.

If the tear does not seal itself immediately, death by strangulation will soon follow. The hematoma will grow larger with each pulsation of the heart and eventually start pressing against the trachea until it has compressed it enough to stimulate the laryngeal nerves to close it off. The outside appearance will be that of a huge swelling on the side of the neck (Fig. 29).

IX. A chipped or fractured SPINOUS PROCESS of the vertebra is one of the most dangerous occurances, not because of the fracture but because of what lies between it and the outside surface of the skin, which in this case is everything previously mentioned in this Chapter. Also there would be the possibility of spinal cord shock (injury to the spinal cord without any known disruption of the spinal cord fibers—*whiplash*).

X. Fracture of the THYROID OR CRICOID CARTILAGE is the result of a frontal blow to the throat. The most important thing to remember here is that surrounding the cartilages are many nerve branches of the larynx (laryngenial nerves). Of course, stimulation of these nerves by a fracture of the cartilage will activate the vocal cords and epiglottis to close off the air supply to the lungs, resulting in a slow death by suffocation or at least unconsciousness from lack of air.

Because of the close proximity of all the above mentioned effects and results, it is easy to see how two or more of the effects would exist and cause death to or at least total disability of the attacker.

9
Striking the Back of the Neck

By pivoting away while you block, you dissipate the force of the blow and prepare for a chop to the neck.

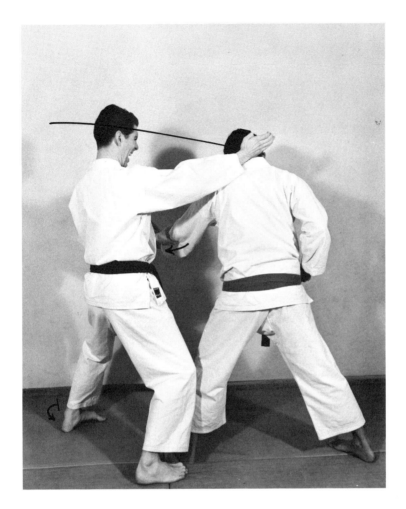

As you start the downward motion of the chop you grab your opponent's arm and pull him slightly forward and off balance, and at the same time you pivot back into a strong stance just as you strike the neck.

This technique was completed in $\frac{7}{10}$ of one second.

WEAPON: Chop (Side of the hand)
TARGET: Back of the neck

Medical Implications

I. Muscle spasms and a WHIPLASH INJURY should be considered the minimum possible damage resulting from this type of blow. There is also a possibility that the blow might result in permanent spinal cord shock (injury to the spinal cord—better known as a whiplash injury). Noticeable symptoms will appear immediately or at a later date. These symptoms occur in many degrees of severity, from constant neck strain (as if a muscle were pulled) and severe headaches, to pains throughout the neck and back area.

CONCUSSIVE VIBRATION

FIG. 32

SPINAL CORD

CUT-AWAY THROUGH MIDDLE OF SPINAL COLUMN

FIG. 33

FRACTURE OF VERTEBRA

PINCHED AND CONTUSED
SPINAL CORD (WITH
BLEEDING IN THE FIBRE)

PINCHED AND COMPRESSED
INTERVERTEBRAL DISC

56

II. A broken neck is the term used to specify a SEVERED SPINAL CORD. This is usually accomplished by the severing action of a fractured vertebra. Complete paralysis from the point of impact downward will result.

If the cord is severed above the fifth cervical vertebra, death will be immediate.

The spinal cord is very much like a multiple strand telephone cable in the sense that it is composed of many nerve strands, and these strands together make up one dense cord. The phrenic nerve is most accessible between the second and fourth vertebrae. If it is severed it will be fatal, because it controls the function of the diaphragm in breathing. Shock, loss of consciousness, coma, and death waste no time in arriving.

III. Multiple FRACTURE OF THE CERVICAL VERTEBRA with bleeding in a pinched spinal cord will cause partial to complete paralysis encompassing any or all portions of the body and limbs below the point of impact. Respiratory paralysis may be due to a compressed phrenic nerve. Death may be immediate or occur later. Inability to move the head from side to side, dizziness and headache are the minimal possibilities from a medium-strength blow.

A CONCUSSION may exist due to the transmission of shock waves through the brain stem into the brain. Shock (caused by too much stress on the nervous system) may by itself cause death. This is sometimes referred to as a violent interruption of the body's homostatic balance.

10
Striking the Collar Bone

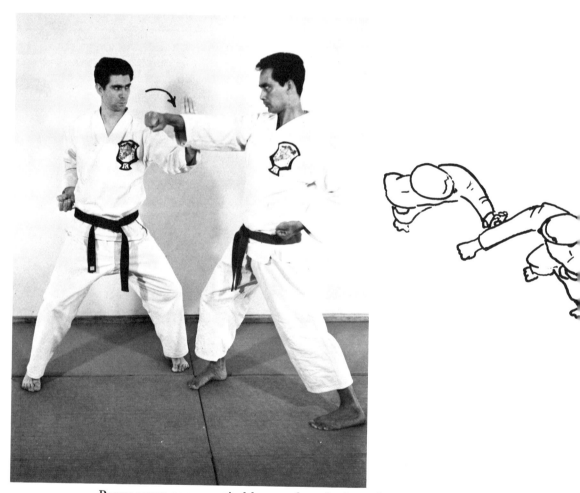

Parry your opponent's blow and cock the other limb in a ready position.

Pull his arm down as you step behind his forward leg and deliver an elbow blow to his collar bone.

This technique was completed in 8/10 of one second.

WEAPON: Elbow
TARGET: Collar Bone (Clavicle)

Medical Implications

I. A FRACTURE OF THE COLLAR BONE (CLAVICLE) would surely disable the opponent's arm on the side of the body the fracture was on. There will be an obvious dropping of the shoulder accompanied by sharp pains.

II. Common complications of the fracture are severance or LACERATION OF THE BRANCHIAL NERVE PLEXUS AND SUBCLAVIAN ARTERY. Severance or laceration of the branchial nerve will cause paralysis

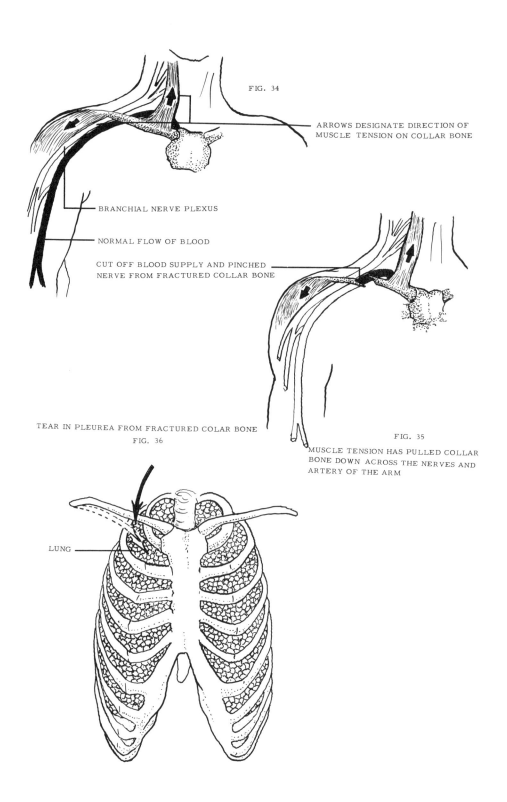

FIG. 34

ARROWS DESIGNATE DIRECTION OF
MUSCLE TENSION ON COLLAR BONE

BRANCHIAL NERVE PLEXUS

NORMAL FLOW OF BLOOD

CUT OFF BLOOD SUPPLY AND PINCHED
NERVE FROM FRACTURED COLLAR BONE

TEAR IN PLEUREA FROM FRACTURED COLAR BONE
FIG. 36

FIG. 35

MUSCLE TENSION HAS PULLED COLLAR
BONE DOWN ACROSS THE NERVES AND
ARTERY OF THE ARM

LUNG

of part or all of the arm. Laceration of the artery is also a common side effect because it follows the nerve closely (under the collar bone, Fig. 34). If the artery was merely pinched (due to muscle tension pulling up and down on the collar bone—Fig. 35) and blood was not allowed to pursue it's normal path through the arm, thrombosis* would occur. The pinched artery must be remedied within four to six hours or the risk of gangrene will be present.

III. If the blow is a heavy one, it can push the jagged edge of the broken bone down far enough to reach the lung. The sharp edges of the break will puncture the plurae (thin sac-like membrane covering the lung) and the lung will gradually deflate. Shortness of breath, air starvation, painful breathing, dizzyness, irregular heart palpitations, unconsciousness, coma and death are the general symptoms of a collapsed lung (Chapter 12, Fig. 42).

* Thrombosis: A Blood clot in the artery, restricting normal flow of blood.)

11
Striking the Solar Plexus

Glance back to see the angle and how far away opponent is, as you do this step forward or back depending on how far away he is.

Counter grab his wrist and pull forward to stretch him out and kick directly to his abdomen with the heel of your foot (toes curled upward for good heel angle).

This technique was completed in $\frac{7}{10}$ of one second.

WEAPON: Heel of the foot
TARGET: Solar Plexus

Medical Implications

As indicated in Figures 38, 39, 40, different angles of the kick will produce varied results. If the kick is directed toward the right side of the opponent's body, the liver and gallbladder will be damaged. If it is in the center of the solar plexus, the duodenum and pancreas will be thrust against the front of the lumbar spine. The abdominal aorta (huge vein) follows the lumbar spine vertically and is very snug against the front side of the vertebra. If the heel kick was strong enough to injure the vein, shock (extreme loss of blood) and death would follow almost immediately. The stomach (and some reports claim that the spleen) will be involved when the blow is to the left side of the solar plexus. The level, angle and strength of the kick will determine how many of these organs will be damaged.

I. A DEEP FISSURE IN THE LIVER may very well be fatal. Peritonitis in the name given to free floating blood and/or bile in the peritoneal cavity (body cavity). Hiccupping from blood or bile irritating the diaphragm

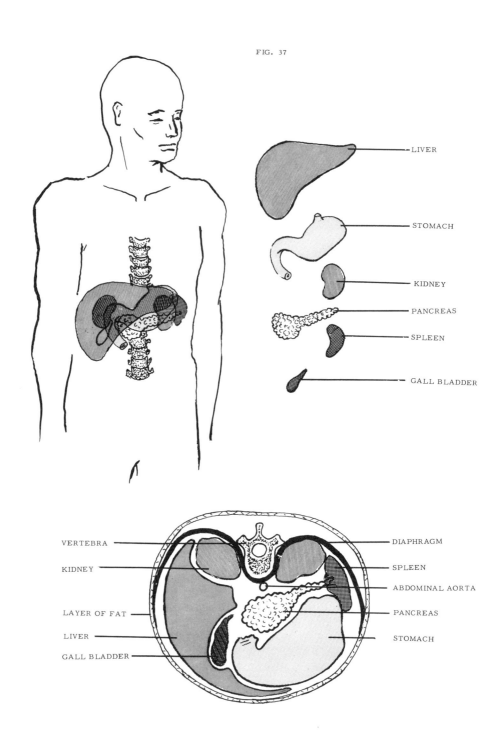

FIG. 37

LIVER

STOMACH

KIDNEY

PANCREAS

SPLEEN

GALL BLADDER

VERTEBRA — — DIAPHRAGM

KIDNEY — — SPLEEN

— ABDOMINAL AORTA

LAYER OF FAT — — PANCREAS

LIVER — — STOMACH

GALL BLADDER —

TOP VIEW OF SOLAR PLEXUS (CUT-AWAY)

TOP VIEWS OF SOLAR PLEXUS (POSSIBLE ANGLES OF PENETRATION)

TEAR IN LIVER AND

GALL BLADDER

HEEL OF FOOT COMPRESSING GALL BLADDER

FIG. 38

COMPRESSION OF PANCREAS
AND ABDOMINAL AORTA
(HUGE VEIN) AGAINST THE
LUMBAR SPINE

SPLIT SURFACE OF
PANCREAS

FIG. 39

NORMAL LINE OF SOLAR PLEXUS

SPLIT SURFACES OF STOMACH

AND DUODENUM

COMPRESSION OF STOMACH AND DUEDEUM

FIG. 40

*ONLY THE NECESSARY ORGANS ARE ILLUSTRATED FOR CLARITY

and an increasing tenderness and pain in the abdomen will continue until surgery of the abdomen corrects the symptoms which may very easily evolve into death.

II. THE GALL BLADDER WOULD BE TORN with gastric acids and digestive juices being spilled into the body cavity. (Prior to a meal, the gall bladder fills with proper digestive juices for digestion of the meal and stores the juices until food is induced. The gall bladder would burst rather easily if enough pressure was exerted upon it during the predigestion period.) The juices would immediately start to digest the internal organs they came in contact with, and only surgery would prevent death.

III. RUPTURE OF THE STOMACH with the spilling of its contents and blood into the body cavity would again result in peritonitis. Days of intestinal disturbances, gastric disorders and vomiting, shock, and eventual death will occur.

IV. A compression injury of the DUODENUM against the lumbar spine will progress the same as III above.

V. AN INJURED PANCREAS may result if the kick were well timed (when the opponent was inhaling) and the solar plexus were relaxed and easily penetrated. The pancreas might also be compressed, along with the duodenum, against the lumbar spine producing a split surface of the organ. Respiratory paralysis (Fig. 45) —spasm of the abdominal and intercostal rib muscles, which inhibits normal movements of the diaphragm in breathing—unconsciousness, shock, and death are the likely results.

VI. PARTIAL COLLAPSE OF THE LUNG (refer to Chapter 12), due to a minute plural tear from the percussive shock (jarring) present in the chest cavity at the moment of impact, will result in shallow breathing and great pain during respiration.

VII. SHOCK is a term used in internal injuries to describe the extreme loss of blood and bile into the body cavity. Shock may be immediately fatal or be latent (48 hours later) until abdominal splinting occurs. Abdominal splinting means that when the cavity fills with blood, it will be evident because of a growing tenderness and increasing rididity of the abdomen, with the elevation of body temperature and possible vomiting of blood from rupture of the stomach or duodenum. Death is the common result of shock, because usually by the time the injured person arrives at the hospital he has lapsed into unconsciousness from lack of blood and cannot tell the doctor his symptoms.

12
Striking the Side of the Rib Cage

Parry and grab (same hand) as you cock your foot ready for heel kick (toes always curled upward).

Pivot away as you pull opponent's arm forward (bringing his weight slightly forward) and execute a heel kick to the middle and side of the ribs.

This technique was completed in $\frac{8}{10}$ of one second.

WEAPON: Heel of foot
TARGET: Side of ribs

Medical Implications

I. A green stick fracture* of the ribs will cause only pain in breathing, but a complete break in the rib, with protruding ends, will tear the lung's pleura (membrane sac covering the lungs) and puncture the lung, resulting in a COLLAPSED LUNG. Blood in the lung cavity (hemothorax) will be present until it is removed. Shortness of breath and muscle spasms

---

* A green stick fracture is when the fracture line runs down the middle of the bone, but does not completely break the continuity of the bone.

LUNG

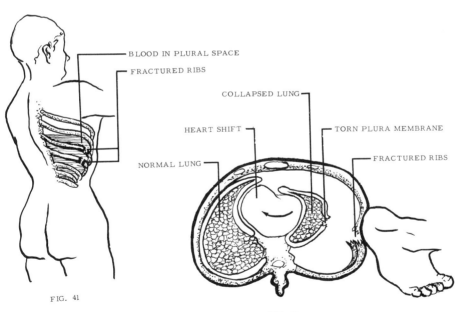

BLOOD IN PLURAL SPACE

FRACTURED RIBS

COLLAPSED LUNG

HEART SHIFT

TORN PLURA MEMBRANE

NORMAL LUNG

FRACTURED RIBS

FIG. 41

FIG. 42
TOP VIEW (CUT-AWAY)

of the chest and rib cage, with severe pain while breathing will predominate. If the lung collapses all the way, death is sure to follow. A lung may be collapsed from the violent jarring produced by the kick, without the presence of a fractured rib. When the pleura tear is very small, it will usually seal itself soon without any great after effects.

The great danger involved with a completely collapsed lung (besides air starvation) is an uncontrollable spasm of the heart, which is caused by the pressure difference when the lung collapses. The heart is held in place (partially) by the lungs on either side and the heart's suspensory ligaments. When there is no pressure on one side to help hold the heart in place, the lung on the other side will pull the heart toward it (heart shift), resulting in a severe muscle spasm of the heart and usually either a quick or lingering death. Intercostal muscle spasms (muscles between the ribs) with loss of breath would be the minimal damage (refer to Chapter 13, Fig. 45). A complication of this blow would be a puncture of the diaphragm (refer to Chapter 13, Fig. 46).

13
Striking the Diaphragm

Position your two fingers directly under the nose (upper lip) and press in and upward. Lever the opponent's head back and down.

Strike down when opponent is stretched back (before he falls down).

This technique was completed in $\frac{7}{10}$ of one second.

WEAPON: Hammerfist
TARGET: Diaphragm

Medical Implications

I. Just a light tap near the lower frontal ribs will cause a slight contraction of the diaphragm and intercostal muscles. The diaphragm's main function is that of respiration. The intercostal muscles (muscles between each rib) take over the function of the diaphragm in situations of stress, but they soon tire and will not function properly. A hard blow to the diaphragm or ribs will relax those muscles and all breathing will cease for the moment because when relaxed, the muscles force the air out of the lungs and continue to squeeze until the muscles let the ribs expand again for inspiration of air.

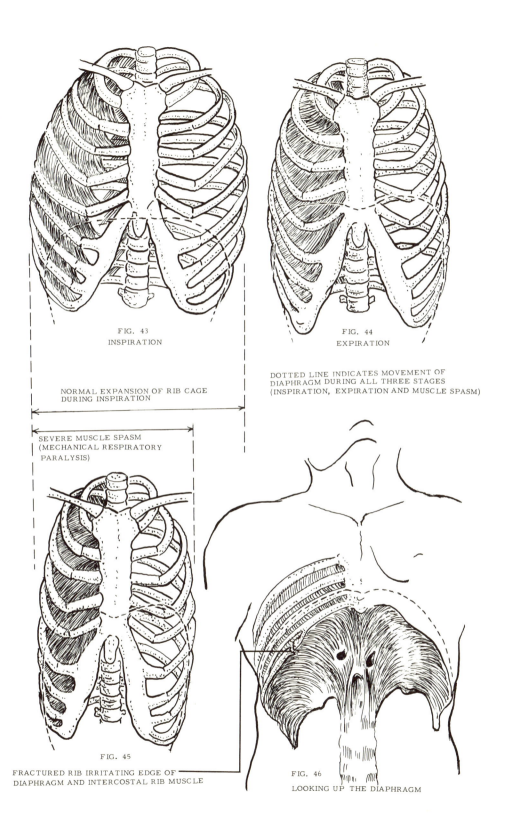

FIG. 43
INSPIRATION

FIG. 44
EXPIRATION

NORMAL EXPANSION OF RIB CAGE
DURING INSPIRATION

DOTTED LINE INDICATES MOVEMENT OF
DIAPHRAGM DURING ALL THREE STAGES
(INSPIRATION, EXPIRATION AND MUSCLE SPASM)

SEVERE MUSCLE SPASM
(MECHANICAL RESPIRATORY
PARALYSIS)

FIG. 45

FRACTURED RIB IRRITATING EDGE OF
DIAPHRAGM AND INTERCOSTAL RIB MUSCLE

FIG. 46
LOOKING UP THE DIAPHRAGM

Unconsciousness, due to a mechanical respiratory paralysis (Fig. 45), is a common result from such a blow.

II. The jagged edge of a fractured rib irritating the surface of the diaphragm will produce "shallow breathing." The diaphragm will move up and down while normal respiration occurs, but when it is stopped by a sharp edge of bone puncturing it, "shallow breathing" (short breaths) occurs. Also blood irritating the diaphragm will cause painful hiccuping. Unconsciousness, coma, and death are the usual results.

14
Striking the Spleen

Step back into a ready position, as you parry the blow.

Grab your opponent's wrist as you pivot away with an instep kick to his side.

This technique was completed in $^{6}/_{10}$ of one second.

WEAPON: Instep of the foot
TARGET: Spleen

Medical Implications

I. The spleen is located on the left side of the rib cage right beside the left kidney, under the diaphragm and parallel to the ninth, tenth and eleventh ribs. The function of the spleen that we are chiefly concerned with here is its ability to act as a reservoir for the storage of blood and to return it to normal circulation in harmony with the body's needs. During shock or fright, blood drains into the spleen and other internal organs. Under normal and stress situations the spleen is partially or nearly totally full of blood (according to the environment and emotions). (The spleen

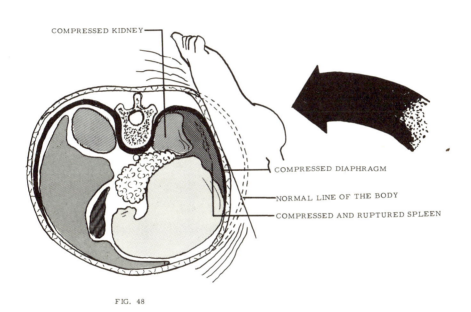

COMPRESSED KIDNEY

COMPRESSED DIAPHRAGM

NORMAL LINE OF THE BODY

COMPRESSED AND RUPTURED SPLEEN

FIG. 48

NOTE: FLOATING RIBS LEFT OUT FOR CLARITY

is also one of the main organs that fights against bodily infection, a very important function.)

II. A fracture of the ribs with lacerations of the diaphragm and spleen is the beginning of a slow but sure death.

Shock due to the loss of blood with weakness, nausea, severe pain and tenderness from the point of impact to the left side of the abdomen are the first symptoms; unconsciousness, coma, and death usually follow within forty-eight hours. Spasm of the diaphragm (Chapter 12) will also be present. Abdominal splinting is the hardening of the abdomen to a board-like ridgity due to the accumulation of a large amount of blood between the muscles and the abdominal cavity. Abdominal splinting will be a symptom in nearly all abdominal injuries. Pain in the abdomen and nausea occurs from the irritation of blood and bile in the abdominal cavity.

III. Even if the ribs are not fractured, a delayed rupture of the spleen may occur any time from within twenty-four hours to two years.* A small fissure or bruise, caused at the time of injury, can eventually increase in size and ultimately result in a massive hemorrhage with death the ultimate end. A delayed rupture of the spleen is almost always fatal because it is unexpected. A blow from the front or side can result in rupture of the spleen, especially if the opponent is inhaling when contact is made. During inhalation the muscles of the trunk are relaxed and very soft. This is evident by the easy pentration of a blow on inhalation.

---

* "Delayed rupture of the spleen" *Archives of Surgery* Vol. 92 No. 3, March 1966, p. 362.

15
Striking the Kidney

Block with one hand as you cock the other.

Just as your body weight plants strike to the side with the tip of your elbow. The parrying hand grabs and pulls opponent slightly forward and down.

This technique was completed in ⁶⁄₁₀ of one second.

WEAPON: Elbow
TARGET: Kidney

Medical Implications

I. Rupture of the kidney, with bleeding in the capsule, can be prevalent with or without broken ribs. Hydrostatic pressure from the impact of the twelfth rib hitting the kidney can cause the rupture.

II. Laceration of the kidney from a broken rib is the most common type of injury from a blow of this nature. There will be peritonitis,* extreme pain,

---

* Peritonitis is an accumulation of blood and urine irritating the abdominal walls— extreme tenderness of the abdomen.

FIG. 49
BLEEDING IN LUNG CAVITY
FRACTURED RIBS

FIG. 50

BLEEDING IN KIDNEY AND KIDNEY CAPSULE

OUTLINE OF THE DIAPHRAGM
KINK IN URETHRAL TUBE
(URINE BLOCKAGE)

FIG. 51
NORMAL KIDNEY AND CAPSULE
WITH ACCESSORY MUSCLE OF
SPINE

FIG. 52
TORN AND DISPLACED
KIDNEY AND CAPSULE
WITH BLEEDING INTO
BODY CAVITY

bloody urination, coma, and death (or at least many weeks in bed).

III. If the blow was a glancing type, just below the last rib (twelfth), the kidney capsule (membrane that holds kidney in place) would be torn from its moorings, causing bleeding into the body cavity; and because the ureter is displaced, a bend or kink in the ureter (urinary tube that goes to the bladder) would result in a urinary blockage, followed by infection and sometimes death.

IV. Because the diaphragm lies between the ribs and kidney, it will also be punctured if a complete break in the ribs has resulted. Spasms of the intercostal rib muscles and diaphragm will result in temporary to permanent respiratory paralysis with severe pain and ultimately death. (Chapter 12, Fig. 45.)

V. When the blow is three or four inches higher it may have an end result equal to that of a collapsed lung.

16

Striking the Elbow

Pin your antagonist's wrist to your lapel

Step in with a forearm blow, just behind his elbow joint

This technique was completed in $\frac{7}{10}$ of one second.

WEAPON: Forearm
TARGET: Elbow

Medical Implications

I. Fracture of the humorus will result when the blow is slightly above the elbow joint. In injuries to the upper arm, the ulna and sometimes the radial and median nerves may be pinched or severed by the broken bone, resulting in slight to permanent paralysis of parts of the arm and/or hand. Nausea, anxiety, and extreme pain accompany this trauma.

II. Injury to the branchial artery in an unwelcome complication of the fracture because a pinched or severed blood vessel may result in tissue damage or gangrene. Four to six hours is all that is needed to produce this condition. Loss of sensation and amputation of the arm is the irreversible outcome.

III. "Tennis elbow" can be a very devastating injury. A torn bursa (lubricating sac of the elbow joint) will cause a swelling of tremendous size in

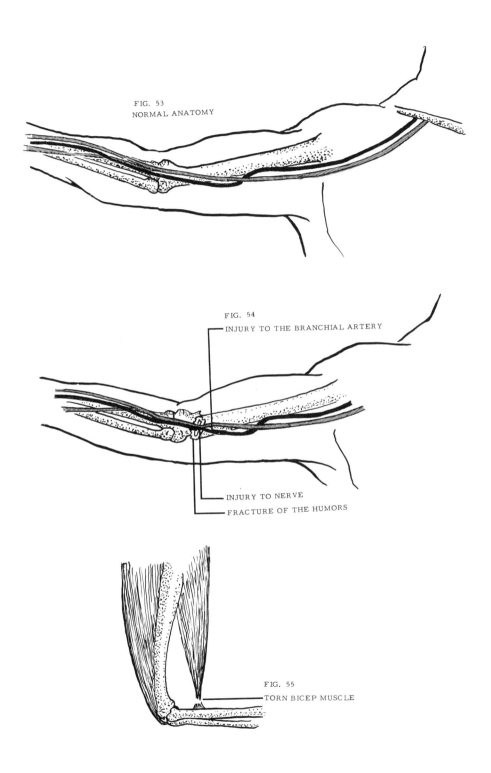

FIG. 53
NORMAL ANATOMY

FIG. 54
INJURY TO THE BRANCHIAL ARTERY

INJURY TO NERVE
FRACTURE OF THE HUMORS

FIG. 55
TORN BICEP MUSCLE

and around the elbow. Extreme pain in the elbow when extension of the arm is attempted is the adhering symptom. Joint motion may be limited because of adhesions within the muscles (biceps, etc.) and tendons surrounding the joint.

17
Striking the Bladder

Block and cock the striking hand ready.

Pull opponent's arm down (to keep him from moving away) and pivot rear foot, as you use the momentum of the pivot to deliver a reverse hammerfist.

This technique was completed in $\frac{7}{10}$ of one second.

WEAPON: Reverse Hammerfist
TARGET: Bladder

Medical Implications

I. Rupture of the urinary bladder in its distended (full) state is equivalent to filling a balloon with air until a weak portion of the balloon ruptures and releases its contents, which in this case is urine. The area of the bladder will have a strained feeling with increasing tenderness from spilled urine and blood in the body cavity. Inability to urinate more than a few bloody drops of urine—if at all—is an indication of a rupture of the bladder or urethral passageway (tube leading from the bladder to the outside). Infec-

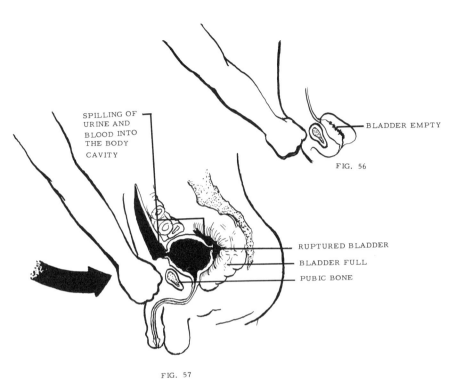

SPILLING OF URINE AND BLOOD INTO THE BODY CAVITY

BLADDER EMPTY

FIG. 56

RUPTURED BLADDER

BLADDER FULL

PUBIC BONE

FIG. 57

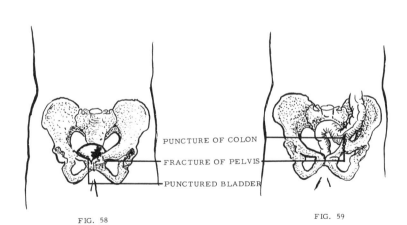

PUNCTURE OF COLON

FRACTURE OF PELVIS

PUNCTURED BLADDER

FIG. 58

FIG. 59

89

INGUINAL AND
FEMORAL RINGS

FEMORAL NERVE
AND VEINS

INGUINAL HERNIA

FEMORAL HERNIA
CAUSING PRESSURE
ON FEMORAL NERVE
AND VEINS

FIG. 60

THROMBOSIS (BLOOD CLOT IN THE VESSEL,
CLOGGING NORMAL CIRCULATION)

FIG. 61

HERNIA

FIG. 62

BLOOD CLOT

tion due to lesions in the tube or bladder cause urinary retention, muscle spasm of the bladder, or painful and frequent urination. Infection seems to be an accomplice of nearly all urinary injuries.

II. A really hard driving blow (slightly lower) would fracture the pubic bone and consequently puncture the bladder (with the same results as above).

III. A fracture of the top edge of the pubic bone may easily produce a punctured colon (intestine) if an off-center blow to the left side of the opponent occurs. Respiration will be difficult because of the pressure downward of the intestinal tract upon the fractured bone segment. Hemorrhage and shock conclude this injury.

IV. Because of the wide area of this blow and the narrowing delta-like region of the lower abdomen, a possible inguinal or femoral hernia may develop if the blow is a few inches lower on either side of the bladder. This occurs basically because of the already weakened and thin inguinal and femoral muscle rings. The inguinal and femoral rings are the byproduct of a number of muscles disecting at various angles to produce a whirlpool effect with a hole in the center.

In the inguinal ring, the spermatic cord (cord leading to the testicle) emerges from this hole. When the surrounding muscle is weakened from a tear or disruption of the muscle fibers, portions of the bowl, bladder, and/or omentum (abdominal membrane) may protrude through the weakened muscle ring and continue into the scrotum (scrotal hernia). This is the usual discomforting after-effect of a strong blow in this region.

V. Two related complications may become prevalent in a femoral hernia. The femoral and iliac vein and the femoral nerve run through or by the ring orifice.

    a.) Protruding parts of the bowl, or omentum, may become constricted from pressure of the expanded ring around them. These parts may become gangrenous from lack of blood. Of course, pressure on the femorial nerve if severe enough will cause partial paralysis of the lower limb.

    b.) Thrombosis* in the femorial vein (depending upon how great the thrombosis) can ultimately lodge in the lungs and cause death.

* Thrombosis: Blood clot in the vessel, clogging circulation.

18

Striking the Groin

Step back into a cat stance (stretching him forward) as you push upward on his elbows to elevate the pressure on your throat.

Push your head back away from his choke, as you use a ball kick to the groin.

This technique was completed in $\frac{7}{10}$ of one second.

WEAPON: Ball of foot
TARGET: Groin

Medical Implications

I. Rupture of the bladder from the percussive jolt of a solid kick or from a fracture of the pubic bone, are the two main methods of rupture (other than the method already mentioned in the previous chapter). Blood and urine in the abdominal cavity will be in abundance with the usual tenderness and pain.

II. The center of the pubic bone is the weakest and most probable place of fracture. An inability to walk because of the nauseating pain originating between the legs (due to the pinching, abrading effect of the separated pubic bones rubbing together upon attempted movement) will leave your opponent in a distressed prone position.

III. In order for the kick to penetrate to the underside of the frontal pubic bone, it must first drive through the penis and scrotum (not a very difficult feat). Disruption of the urethra (urinary tube leading to the outside) with

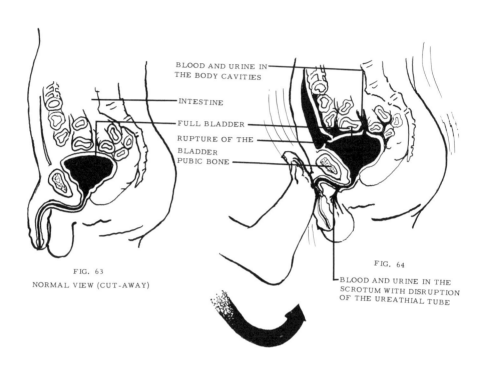

BLOOD AND URINE IN
THE BODY CAVITIES

INTESTINE

FULL BLADDER

RUPTURE OF THE
BLADDER

PUBIC BONE

FIG. 63

NORMAL VIEW (CUT-AWAY)

FIG. 64

BLOOD AND URINE IN THE
SCROTUM WITH DISRUPTION
OF THE UREATHIAL TUBE

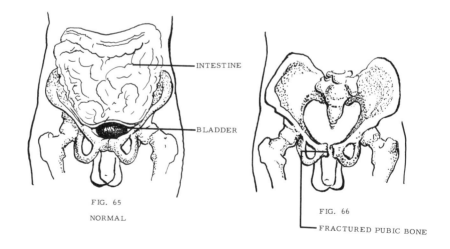

INTESTINE

BLADDER

FIG. 65

NORMAL

FIG. 66

FRACTURED PUBIC BONE

bleeding and urine into the scrotum will be the minimal injury. Bloody and painful urination or an inability to urinate will more than likely be the aftermath.

IV. The testicles are extremely mobile within the loose skin of the scrotum; however, a crushed testicle may result, due to the wide surface of the ball of the foot striking it. Sterility to one or both testicles is one sure occurrence from such a heavy blow. Pain, shock, loss of breath, nausea, vomiting, unconsciousness (and sometimes death) commonly follow one another.

19
Striking the Spine

Step back and cock elbow ready to strike down.

While you are still in a solid position, strike down to spine.

This technique was completed in $^4/_{10}$ of one second.

WEAPON: Elbow
TARGET: Spine

Medical Implications

I. A fracture of the thoracic vertebra and intervertebral disc will quickly neutralize your opponent. Paralysis of the body below the point of impact will predominate if the crushed vertebra or disc has severed or created enough direct pressure to compress the spinal cord. Loss of control of the bladder and rectum from paralysis is a distressing adjustment. The higher up on the spine the blow was struck, the more areas involved in paralysis. Quite often urinary infection results because of the paralyzed bladder.

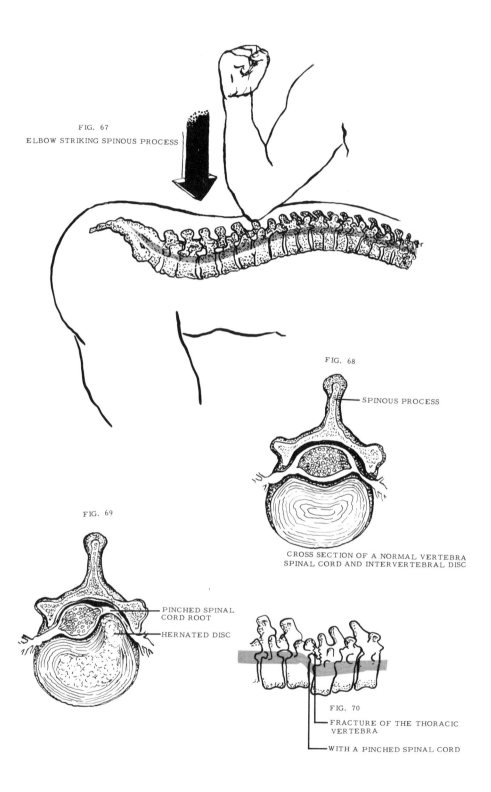

FIG. 67
ELBOW STRIKING SPINOUS PROCESS

FIG. 68

SPINOUS PROCESS

CROSS SECTION OF A NORMAL VERTEBRA
SPINAL CORD AND INTERVERTEBRAL DISC

FIG. 69

PINCHED SPINAL
CORD ROOT

HERNATED DISC

FIG. 70
FRACTURE OF THE THORACIC
VERTEBRA

WITH A PINCHED SPINAL CORD

II. Pressure in the spinal cord due to a hemorrhage there may produce partial to complete paralysis (without the presence of a crushed vertebra or disc exerting pressure upon the cord).

III. Minor results, if you have withheld the force of the blow, will be a pinched nerve root (nerve strand leaving the vertebra and connecting to any number of muscle or organ groups throughout the body) causing slight paralysis and malfunction of certain areas. This is often termed a slipped disc or herniated disc (Figure 69). Extrusion of the disc (herniated disc) into the region of the cord may terminate in partial to complete motor and/or sensory loss or uncontrollable spastic movement. This may be a later effect.

IV. Spinal cord shock ("whiplash"), without visible disruption of the cord fibers, will radiate violent pain up and down the spinal cord.

V. If the blow slipped off or missed the vertebra by a fraction of an inch and struck hard, it would easily collapse the lung (Chapter 12) from the percussive shock of the blow or from a fractured rib.

20
Striking the Thigh

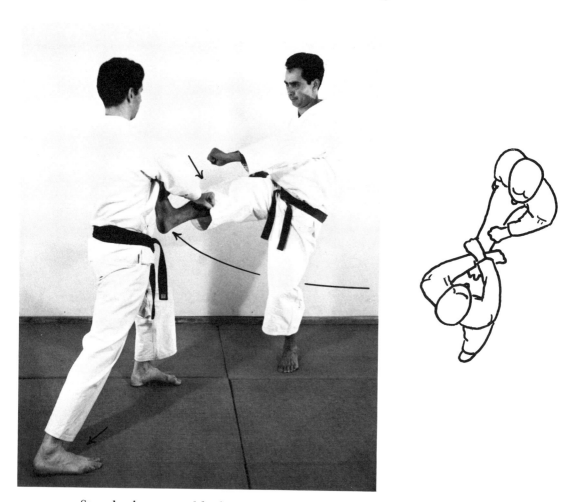

Step back as you block cross handed and immediately clamp your hands around his ankle.

Pull straight up as you pivot your front foot and deliver a knee raise to the underside of his thigh. Your right hand pushes down as your knee strikes the under side of his thigh.

This technique was completed in $\frac{8}{10}$ of one second.

WEAPON: Knee
TARGET: Underside of the thigh

Medical Implications

I. This technique is one that should be used only when the attacker has demonstrated an inadequate attempt to deliver a slow or sloppy kick. Ultimately, this blow (one of the strongest human weapons) will fracture or dislocate the femur. The result is severe: many months in a fracture bed with immediate immobility and possible shock because of the harsh pain. Severe muscle spasm (Figure 75) will be prevalent with any hard blow to a muscle.

FIG. 71
DISLOCATION OF THE FEMUR

FIG. 72
FRACTURE OF THE FEMUR

FIG. 73
TORN MUSCLE SHEATH
(THIN MEMBRANE-LIKE COVERING OF THE MUSCLE)

FIG. 74
MYTOMA

BLOOD IN MUSCLE
TISSUE

FIG. 75

LENGTH OF NORMAL
MUSCLE FIBERS

LENGTH OF MUSCLE IN
VIOLENT SPASM

II. Disruption of the muscle sheath and bleeding in the muscle fibre (mytoma) are the common outcome. Herniation of the muscle tissues is a result of the torn muscle sheath (thin membrane covering) that normally covers and binds the muscle groups and fibers together. Without the restricting pressure of the membrane around the muscle, a protrusion of the injured muscle fibre through the torn membrane will create a lump on the point of impact. Many months of immobility due to loss of contracting ability of the muscle are sure to follow.

21

Striking the Back of the Knee

Step forward to the side as you double parry opponent's punch.

Hold onto his arm and shoulder for stability as you pivot and use a knife thrust to the back of the rear knee (use side of foot, toes upward).

This technique was completed in $\frac{8}{10}$ of one second.

WEAPON: Knife edge of foot
TARGET: Back of knee

Medical Implications

I. The popliteal blood vessels and tabialis nerve run together up and down the backside of the leg, so when one is affected the other usually is also. A torn blood vessel and abrasion of the nerve can easily result from a kick of this nature (especially when a shoe is worn). A large hematoma (an organized area of blood spilled from a torn blood vessel) will form under the skin and sometimes the swelling will extend forward to the front of the knee. An abrasion of the nerve will cause partial paralysis of the leg below the point of impact; the mobility of the knee will be greatly impaired to say the least.

II. When the knee is thrust forward and the upper body is jerked back, the muscle tension on the knee is so great that it can tear all of the muscles of the knee; often the muscle action has torn the kneecap in half. Repair of such violent trauma is major in effect and must be done soon or the

PATELLA (KNEE CAP)
TORN IN HALF FROM
MUSCLE TENSION

FIG. 76
SKIN REMOVED
FOR CLARITY

FIG. 77

DISLOCATION OF
THE KNEE

TORN LIGAMENT

PINCHED NERVE

FIG. 78
LARGE HEMATOMA
(BLOOD CLOT)

FIG. 79
TORN PATELLA LIGAMENT
TORN LATERAL LIGAMENT

muscles will not grow back in the proper places. The great pain and torn muscles will render your opponent virtually helpless.

III. If a dislocation of the knee joint has occurred, it would undoubtedly be the most painful result that could happen to the knee. Surgical repositioning of the ripped muscles and ligaments are a necessary course of action if that individual ever wishes to walk again. Shock, nausea, and pain are the immediate effect.

22

Striking the Front Knee Joint

Step back as you parry and grab your opponent's arm (for balance).

Pull opponent slightly forward (to shift his weight onto his front foot) and thrust with the side of your foot to his knee (toes curled upward, for better angle and control).

This technique was completed in $\frac{7}{10}$ of one second.

WEAPON: Knife thrust (side of the foot)
TARGET: The side of the knee joint

Medical Implications

I. A LIGHT TO HEAVY SPRAIN will cause a tender or strained sensation in the knee joint, which is a result of the muscles and ligaments being stretched to their maximum elasticity. There will be painful movement and stiffness of the knee joint for quite some time.

II. SURFACE LACERATIONS (ABRASIONS) of the skin will occur if you are wearing hard soled shoes when you are attacked.

FIG. 80

BONE ATTACHED TO LIGAMENT

TORN LIGAMENT

NORMAL SEMI-LUNAR CARTILAGE

TORN SEMI-LUNAR CARTILAGE

FIG. 82

SWELLING OF THE KNEE

TORN (BURSA) LUBRICATING
SAC OF THE KNEE JOINT

FIG. 81

III. RUPTURED BLOOD VESSELS should be a result regardless of the strength of the kick. The larger vessels would be broken if it were a very forceful blow. There would be a large balloon or walnut like deformity (hematoma) pushing out wherever the blood vessel was torn.

IV. A TORN BURSA (lubricating sac that covers the lining of the knee joint) will occur very easily if it were pinched or abraded against any portion of the nearby bone surface, thus spilling the lubricating fluid under the skin and creating the usual grotesque, lumpy, or swollen appearance extending from the front to the back of the knee.

V. ABRADED AND TORN SEMI-LUNAR CARTILAGE is one of the most painful results that would follow (especially if the attacker had most of his weight on the forward foot and the knee was relatively straight at the moment of impact). This will come about by one bone grinding across the other in a sharp digging manner. The semi-lunar cartilage is the cushion of the knee joint. It aids in the smooth movement that exists when you walk or stoop down to pick up something from the floor. If the injury were bad enough, it could require surgical removal and/or repositioning of the cartilage fragments.

VI. AN AVULSION FRACTURE WITH TORN LIGAMENTS represents probably the most pictorial result that we can illustrate easily. If you will imagine a wire cable being plastered to a wall and then ripped loose after it was dried, consequently pulling a large chunk of attached plaster with it, then you can guess the painful results when a ligament has been ripped loose, pulling with it the bony insertion that normally adheres to the thigh bone (femur). This is possible when your foot hits above the joint and continues to scrape down the outside surface of the knee joint until it strikes the natural depression made by the two connecting bones (tibia and femur) and rips the ligament from its fixed position.

23
Striking the Shin Bone

Shift your weight onto your rear foot and cock your front foot inside your right knee (toes curled downward for better angle on a snapping knife edge kick to a low target such as the shin).

This technique was completed in $\frac{4}{10}$ of one second.

WEAPON: Side of foot
TARGET: Shin bone

Medical Implications

I. Without a shoe, it is doubtful a complete break in the tibia or fibula will occur. But, if the kick is done with a hard soled shoe, it will easily fracture one or both bones of the lower limb, depending on the angle and solidity of the opponent's limb just prior to contact of the kick. The fracture is sometimes compounded soon after injury by the person's effort to stand and walk. If only one bone is fractured, the other bone will act as a splint, and, if the fracture is not a severe one, slight pressure can be applied

FIG. 83
COMPLETE FRACTURE
OF THE TIBIA AND FIBULA

BREAK IN BONE AND MARROW
INJURED MUSCLE FIBERS
TINY BONE FRAGMENTS FLOATING IN SPILLED BLOOD
HEMATOMA (BROKEN BLOOD VESSELS)

BLOW UP OF FRACTURED BONE
FIG. 84

(with great pain) for balance with most of the weight on the uninjured leg. Nauseating pain and inability to exert the slightest degree of pressure on the limb are companions of a complete fracture of the tibia and fibula.

II. A large area of blood spilled from the many torn blood vessels (hematoma) will form around the fracture site and create a huge swelling of the lower limb (Figure 84).

III. "Arterial embolism" is any abnormal particle carried in the vessel which becomes lodged in a vessel too small to permit its passage. The particles may be identified as a blood clot from another part of the body, fat, bacteria, bile or missils (bone) which cause circulatory failure of a section of the body, gangrene, or ultimately death.

In the case of a severe fracture of the shin where there are many tiny bone splinters, and many disrupted particles of fat (that normally lie between the layers of skin) there is a good possibility of these tiny particles finding their way into a torn blood vessel and lodging in a narrow part of the vessel. This is a threat whenever a bone has shattered into many fragments.

24

Striking the Achilles Tendon

As you parry opponent's punch, grab his arm (for balance and control of opponent) and collapse the back of his knee all the way to the ground with the side of your foot.

Shift your left hand to his shoulder (so that he will not fall out of range), plant your left foot on the ground, and stomp to his heel with your right foot.

As you stomp with your right foot, lift your left foot up so that all of your weight is on your right foot, and the pressure is concentrated straight down onto opponent's heel.

This technique was completed in 8/10 of one second.

WEAPON: Bottom of Foot
TARGET: Achilles tendon

Medical Implications

I. A sprained ankle is the least traumatic injury caused by a stomp with the foot in this position. Sprains are partially or completely torn ligaments, tendons and muscles. Sometimes they are just stretched to their limit and cause a great deal of ache and sharp pains when light pressure is applied.

FRACTURE OF FIBIA

TORN MEDIAL LIGAMENT

FIG. 85

FIG. 86

ACHILLES TENDON

FRACTURE OF TARIS

FRACTURE OF THE
METATARSELS

FIG. 87
BACKWARD DISLOCATION OF FOOT

II. Any combination of fractures of the tibia, fibula, tarsus and metatarsals (bones of the foot and ankle) will be present when the blow is struck with full force. An extreme swelling (hematoma) from many lacerated veins will grow so big as to make setting of the broken bones very difficult to manipulate into their original positions. Walking on the injured foot will be an impossiblity. Shock, nausea, and vomiting with possible loss of consciousness are immediate possibilities.

III. Backward dislocation of the foot (Fig. 87) is possible when the blow strikes the upper portion of the ankle. The tibia and fibula are thrust down toward the ground, virtually leaving the rest of the foot in its vertical position. The achilles tendon and many other ligaments and muscles will be ripped away from their fixed positions.

Shock

The term SHOCK will be present in a great many of the sections. Defining shock is not a simple task because much is known about it, but much is yet undiscovered. I will touch on only four closely related types of shock: (1) wound shock (2) hemorrhagic shock (3) septic shock (4) neurogenic shock.

(1) WOUND SHOCK may include all open type of wounds which result in CIRCULATORY FAILURE due to severe injury.

(2) HEMORRHAGIC SHOCK is generally a massive internal hemorrhage (loss of blood and plasma) with minimal injury. This usually refers to a key blood vessel that does not seal itself but continues to leak blood and plasma under the skin or into the body cavity without any immediate symptoms. Weakness, shortness of breath, cold and clammy skin, sweating, greyness of the skin (pallor), thirst (due to the salivary glands ceasing to perform in their normal function), coma, and death can occur within twenty-four hours.

(3) SEPTIC SHOCK is circulatory failure due to a host of infections. This is a later complication of injury (days or weeks after the initial injury).

(4) NEUROGENIC SHOCK is the most complicated of all types to define because it is a product of environment (society) and unpleasant past experiences (traumatic experiences). Slowing of the heart with a decrease in blood pressure (circulatory failure) when hearing unpleasant tidings and seeing objects of horror or the flow of blood, etc., is a social or individual development and usually ends with unconsciousness.

In summary, shock stems from either direct or indirect circulatory failure. Direct circulatory failure pertaining to the physical self (physical wound) and indirect circulatory failure pertaining to the mental self (psychologic trauma).

Death to the individual results when enough vital cells have died. Thus, an individual may die of anoxia (inadequate supply of oxygen) or uremia (toxic presence of urinary constituents in the blood) many days after all signs of shock have disappeared; or he may die of irreparable brain damage despite normal treatment for shock.

Bibliography

CHAPTER 1. a. *A Compilation of Paintings on Normal and Pathological Nervous Systems, With a Supplement on the Hypothalmus,* Vol. I. Frank H. Netter, Summit, N. J. CIBA Pharmaceutical Products Inc. 2nd Edition, Section 5.

b. *Callander's Surgical Anatomy* by Barry J. Anson and Walter G. Maddock. Philadelphia, W. B. Saunders. Chapter 1, 4th Edition.

c. Cunningham's *Textbook of Anatomy,* Tenth Edition, London Oxford University Press, New York, Toronto. (Facial Nerve).

d. *Atlas of Human Anatomy: Simplified,* by Gaynor Evans. Littlefield, Adams and Co., Patterson, N. J. Chapter 3.

CHAPTER 2. a. *Callander's Surgical Anatomy,* Chapters 2 and 3, 3rd Edition, Chapter 2, 4th Edition.

b. *Atlas of Human Anatomy: Simplified,* Chapter 7.

CHAPTER 3. a. *Callander's Surgical Anatomy,* Chapters 1 and 2, 4th Edition.

b. *A Compilation of Paintings on Normal and Pathological Nervous Systems, With a Supplement on the Hypothalmus,* Vol. I, 2nd Edition, Section 2.

c. *An Atlas of Head and Neck Surgery,* John M. Lore, Jr., MD. Saunders Co. Philadelphia & London. Section 5.

d. *Cunningham's Textbook of Anatomy,* 10th Edition. London, New York, Toronto, Oxford University Press. "The Skull," "The Blood, Vascular and Lymphatic Systems," "Arteries of the Head and Neck."

CHAPTER 4. a. *Callander's Surgical Anatomy* by Barry J. Anson and Walter G. Maddock. Philadelphia, W. B. Saunders. 4th Edition, Chapter 1.

CHAPTER 5. a. *Cunningham's Textbook of Anatomy,* Tenth Edition, pages 693–695.

b. *Fundamentals of Otolaryngology* by Lawrence R. Boies, MD. 3rd Edition, Saunders Co. Pages 289–290.

c. *An Atlas of Head and Neck Surgery*, Section 4.

CHAPTER 6. a. *Fundamentals of Otolaryngology* 3rd Edition, Page 288.

b. *Callander's Surgical Anatomy*, 3rd Edition, Chapter 1.

CHAPTER 7. a. *Fundamentals of Otolaryngology*, 3rd Edition, Pages 287–288.

b. *An Atlas of Head and Neck Surgery*, Section 5.

c. *Callander's Surgical Anatomy*, 4th Edition, Chapter 3.

d. *Christopher's Textbook of Surgery*, W. B. Saunders Co. Philadelphia & London. 7th Edition. Page 278.

e. *Cunningham's Textbook of Anatomy*, 10th Edition, Chapter 11.

CHAPTER 8. a. *Management of Fractures and Dislocation: an Atlas* zy Anthony S. De Plama. Philadelphia, W. B. Saunders Co. Vol. I, Part #1.

b. *Fundamentals of Otolaryngology* Pages 323, 389, 393.

c. *Callander's Surgical Anatomy*, 4th Edition, Chapters 7, 8 and 9.

d. *Cunningham's Textbook of Anatomy*, 10th Edition. "The Peripheral Nervous System," "The Digestive System."

e. *Christophers Textbook of Surgery*, 8th Edition, Chapter #10.

CHAPTER 9. a. *A Compilation of Paintings on Normal and Pathological Nervous Systems, With a Supplement on the Hypothalmus*, 2nd Edition, Section #5.

b. *Management of Fractures and Dislocation: an Atlas*, Vol. I, Part 1.

c. *Callander's Surgical Anatomy*, 4th Edition, Chapters 8 and 26.

CHAPTER 10. a. *Callander's Surgical Anatomy*, 4th Edition, Chapters 8 and 27.

b. *Management of Fractures and Dislocations: an Atlas*, Vol. I, Part 1.

c. *Cunningham's Textbook of Anatomy*, 10th Edition, "The Peripheral Nervous System."

CHAPTER 11. a. *Cunningham's Textbook of Anatomy*, 10th Edition,

b. *Christopher's Textbook of Surgery*, 8th Edition, Chapters 4, 15, 17, 18 and 19.

c. *Callander's Surgical Anatomy*, 8th Edition, Chapter 15.

CHAPTER 12. a. *Management of Fractures and Dislocations: an Atlas*, Vol. 1, Parts 1 and 2.

b. *Callander's Surgical Anatomy*, 4th Edition, Chapter 12.

c. *Cunningham's Textbook of Anatomy*, 10th Edition, "The Respiratory System."

CHAPTER 13. a. *Callander's Surgical Anatomy*, 4th Edition, Chapter 15.

b. *Cunningham's Textbook of Anatomy*, 10th Edition, "Myology."

CHAPTER 14. a. *Archives of Surgery*, Vol. 92, No. 3, March 1966, Page 362. "Delayed Rupture of the Spleen."

b. *Christopher's Textbook of Surgery*, Chapter 21.

c. *Cunningham's Textbook of Anatomy*, 10th Edition, "The Blood, Vascular and Lymphatic Systems."

CHAPTER 15. a. *Cunningham's Textbook of Anatomy*, 10th Edition, "The Urogenital System."

b. *Callander's Surgical Anatomy,* 4th Edition, Chapters 14 and 15.

c. *Christophers Textbook of Surgery,* 8th Edition, Chapter 22.

CHAPTER 16. a. *Management of Fractures and Dislocations: an Atlas,* Vol. I, Parts 1 and 2.

CHAPTER 17. a. *Management of Fractures and Dislocations: an Atlas,* Vol. I, Part 1.

b. *Callander's Surgical Anatomy,* 4th Edition, Chapters 16 and 17.

c. *Christophers Textbook of Surgery,* 8th Edition, Chapters 16 and 22.

d. *Atlas of Human Anatomy: Simplified,* Chapter 8.

CHAPTER 18. a. *Callander's Surgical Anatomy,* 4th Edition, Chapters 16 and 18.

b. *Christophers Textbook of Surgery,* 8th Edition, Chapter 23.

CHAPTER 19. a. *A Compilation of Paintings on Normal and Pathological Nervous Systems With a Supplement on the Hypothalmus,* Vol. I, Section 5.

b. *Management of Fractures and Dislocations: an Atlas,* Vol. I, Part 1.

c. *Callander's Surgical Anatomy,* 4th Edition, Chapters 36 and 37.

CHAPTER 20. a. *Management of Fractures and Dislocations: an Atlas,* Vol. II, Part 2.

b. *Callander's Surgical Anatomy,* 4th Edition, Chapters 36 and 37.

CHAPTER 21. a. *Management of Fractures and Dislocations: an Atlas,* Vol. II, Part 2.

b. *Callander's Surgical Anatomy,* 4th Edition, Part 35.

c. *Management of Fractures and Dislocations: an Atlas,* Vol. I, Part 1.

d. *Christophers Textbook of Surgery,* 8th Edition, Chapter 25.

CHAPTER 22. a. *Management of Fractures and Dislocations: an Atlas,* Vol. II, Part 2.

b. *Callander's Surgical Anatomy,* 4th Edition, Chapter 35.

c. *Christophers Textbook of Surgery,* 8th Edition, Chapter 25.

CHAPTER 23. a. *Management of Fractures and Dislocations: an Atlas,* Vol. II, Part 2, Vol. I, Part 2.

b. *Callander's Surgical Anatomy,* 3rd Edition, Chapter 31.

c. *Christophers Textbook of Surgery,* 8th Edition. "Arterial Embolism."

CHAPTER 24. a. *Callander's Surgical Anatomy,* 4th Edition, Chapter 39.

b. *Management of Fractures and Dislocations: an Atlas,* Vol. II, Part 2 and Vol. I, Part 1.

Index